孔子学院总部 /
国家汉办汉语国际推广成都基地规划教材

走进天府系列教材【成都印象】

绣蜀绣

Stitching Shu Embroidery

西 南 财 经 大 学
汉语国际推广成都基地   著

西南财经大学出版社
中国·成都

西 南 财 经 大 学
汉语国际推广成都基地　著

总策划　涂文涛

策　划

李永强

主　编

梁　婷　白巧燕

编　者

《成都印象·游成都》　胡倩琳

《成都印象·居成都》　郑　莹

《成都印象·吃川菜》　谢　娟　王　新

《成都印象·品川茶》　肖　静

《成都印象·饮川酒》　谢　娟

《成都印象·看川剧》　郑　莹

《成都印象·绣蜀绣》　谢　娟

《成都印象·梦三国之蜀国》　蒋林益　胡佩迦

《成都印象·悟道教》　沙　莎　吕　彦　陈　茉

《成都印象·练武术》　邓　帆　刘　亚

审　订　冯卫东

英文翻译

Alexander Demmelhuber

Introduction

If you bring up Sichuanese specialties, there is an innumerous amount that comes to mind: pandas, hot pot, Sichuan opera, Sichuan tea. Among all of them, both Shu brocade and Shu embroidery are the cream of the crop. Many people from other countries come to Sichuan for its famous specialties, but how many people know about Shu brocade? Or Shu embroidery?

This book will introduce its readers to Shu brocade by explaining what Shu brocade is, the relationship between Shu brocade and Chengdu, Shu brocade looms, the history of Shu brocade, and Shu brocade products. This book will also inform its readers about the concept of Shu embroidery, stitching methods, the craft of double-sided embroidery, and so on. As one part of the "Into the Land of Plenty Teaching Series – Impressions of Chengdu", this book follows the "Outline Vocabulary of the New HSK" and the lessons contained herein are designed accordingly. It is suitable for readers at the HSK 5 level.

We hope that you will like *Stitching Shu Embroidery* and we are looking forward to your opinions and suggestions. Hanban gave us much help and support during editing of this book and we would like to take this opportunity to express our gratitude.

前言

说起四川的特产，熊猫、火锅、川剧、川茶……多不胜数，不过，蜀锦蜀绣始终是四川特产里浓墨重彩的一笔。许多外国人为四川特产慕名而来，却很少有人了解何为蜀锦、何为蜀绣。

关于蜀锦，本书介绍了什么是蜀锦、蜀锦与成都、蜀锦织机、蜀锦的历史、蜀锦品种；在蜀绣一章中介绍了蜀绣的概念、针法、双面绣工艺等内容。书中人物均以西南财经大学留学生为原型进行改编创作，所选故事情节丰富实用，语言幽默易懂。

作为《走进天府系列教材·成都印象》中的一本，本书所使用词汇参照《新汉语水平考试词汇大纲》等级编排设计，适合具有HSK5级水平的读者阅读。希望您能喜欢我们的《绣蜀绣》这本教材，也希望您对本书提出批评和建议。本书的编写得到了国家汉办的大力支持和帮助，在此一并表示感谢。

目录

第一课 【关于"锦"的想象】
Lesson 1 【About Brocade as a Phenomenon】

（场景：文小西和江一华在宿舍学习，文小西正用词典查汉字）

① 锦衣玉食　jǐnyī yùshí
② 衣锦还乡　yījǐn huánxiāng
③ 繁花似锦　fánhuā sìjǐn
④ 锦瑟年华　jǐnsè niánhuá
⑤ 昂　贵　ángguì
⑥ 以……为荣　yǐ … wéi róng
⑦ 像……一样　xiàng … yí yàng
⑧ 奢　华　shēhuá
⑨ 精　致　jīngzhì
⑩ 夸　耀　kuāyào
⑪ 奢　侈　shēchǐ
⑫ 象　征　xiàngzhēng
⑬ 向　往　xiàngwǎng

大 萌：
文小西，我今天要考考你们。

文小西：
考什么？

大 萌：
考成语。

文小西：
你说吧。

大 萌：
"锦衣玉食、衣锦还乡"，还有"繁花似锦、锦瑟年华……"

江一华：
为什么都有一个"锦"字？

文小西：
"锦"是什么？

大萌：

"锦"是一种昂贵的丝织品，因为它昂贵又精美，古时候的人都以穿锦衣为荣。"锦衣玉食"的意思是衣服像锦一样华美，食物像玉一样珍贵，形容一种奢华而且精致的生活。一个人富贵以后穿着锦衣回到故乡向亲友夸耀，叫作"衣锦还乡"。

江一华：

所以古时候人们把"锦"当成了奢侈、富贵的象征？

大萌：

是的。"繁花似锦"说的是花儿漂亮得像锦一样。"锦瑟年华"代表人生中最美好的青春年华。

江一华：

所以这里的"锦"意思是美好、漂亮的意思吗？

大萌：

对。"锦"作为一种奢侈品，是普通百姓买不起却又非常向往拥有的东西，在他们的想象中"锦"就是富贵，就是美好，于是他们把一切富贵而美好的东西都用"锦"来形容。

(Scene: Wen Xiaoxi and Jiang Yihua are studying at their dormitory. Wen Xiaoxi is looking up words in her Chinese dictionary)

Da Meng: Wen Xiaoxi, I'd like to test you two today.

Wen Xiaoxi: About what?

Da Meng: Idioms.

Wen Xiaoxi: Shoot.

Da Meng: "Brocade garments, jade meals, return home in brocade garment" and also "flowers in full bloom, brilliant as brocade, the brocade years of youth"…

Jiang Yihua: What's with all the "brocade"?

Wen Xiaoxi: What is this "brocade" ? Although I don't get it, it does sound amazing!

Da Meng: "Brocade" is an expensive silk product. Because it is both expensive and elegant, people in ancient times took pride in wearing brocade clothing. "Brocade garments, jade meals" describes clothing as resplendent as brocade and food as precious as jade, portraying a luxurious and sophisticated life. If somebody becomes rich, returns to their hometown and flaunts their wealth in front of their relatives and friends, this person is said "to return home in brocade garments".

Jiang Yihua: So for the people in ancient times, "brocade" was a symbol of luxury and wealth?

Da Meng: Correct. "Flowers in full bloom, brilliant as brocade" describes flowers that are as beautiful as brocade. "The brocade years of youth" refers to the wonderful years of youth of people's lives.

Jiang Yihua: So "brocade" here means magnificent or beautiful?

Da Meng: Right. "Brocade" was a luxury good. It's something that ordinary people couldn't afford but desperately wanted to possess. To them, "brocade" represented wealth and magnificence. Consequently, they used "brocade" to describe all things expensive and magnificent.

词 语

繁花似锦

繁 花 似 锦

fáhuā-sìjǐn
flowers in full bloom, brilliant as brocade; a blossoming field; a flourishing scene of prosperity

jǐn yī yù shí 锦 衣 玉 食	Brocade garments, jade meals; a life of luxury	yī jǐn huánxiāng 衣 锦 还 乡	go back to one's hometown in brocade robes; return home after acquiring wealth and honor
jǐn sè nián huá 锦 瑟 年 华	age as dignified as brocade; the brocade years of life	áng guì 昂 贵	expensive; costly
shē huá 奢 华	luxurious; sumptuous; lavish	jīng zhì 精 致	delicate; fine; exquisite; refined
kuā yào 夸 耀	brag about; show off; flaunt	shē chǐ 奢 侈	luxurious; extravagant; wasteful
xiàngzhēng 象 征	symbol; symbolize; stand for	xiàng wǎng 向 往	yearn for; look forward to

语言点

1. 以……为荣　　　2. 像……一样

思考

1. 你还知道哪些和锦有关系的成语？把它们找出来吧。

2. 你见过蜀锦吗？在你的国家有跟"锦"类似的东西吗？

请介绍一下。

第二课 【蜀锦是什么】
Lesson 2 【What Is Shu Brocade?】

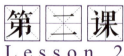

文小西:

为什么四川的锦叫"蜀锦"？

大 萌:

因为"蜀"是四川的别称。

江一华:

"蜀"字里面还有一只"虫"，为什么给四川选这样一个字？

大 萌:

"蜀"是一种古老的蚕虫类。因为古蜀王教四川人种桑养蚕，使四川成为最早的养家蚕的地方，四川也因此扬名天下，所以四川就用"蜀"作别称了。

江一华:

古蜀王为什么会选择四川发展蚕桑业？

① 别称　　　biéchēng
② 蚕虫类　　cán-chóng lèi
③ 桑　　　　sāng
④ 扬名天下　yángmíng tiānxià
⑤ 蚕桑业　　cánsāngyè
⑥ 天府之国　tiānfǔ zhīguó
⑦ 适宜　　　shìyí
⑧ 肥沃　　　féiwò
⑨ 促使　　　cùshǐ
⑩ 纺织业　　fǎngzhīyè
⑪ 美誉　　　měiyù
⑫ 使……成为 shǐ … chéngwéi
⑬ 被称为　　bèi chēngwéi

① 蚕　　　　　cán
② 茧　　　　　jiǎn
③ 启 发　　　qǐfā
④ 织 锦　　　zhī jǐn
⑤ 改 进　　　gǎijìn
⑥ 工 艺　　　gōngyì
⑦ 壮 大　　　zhuàngdà
⑧ 经向彩条　 jīngxiàng cǎitiáo
⑨ 彩条添花　 cǎitiáo tiānhuā
⑩ 悠 久　　　yōujiǔ
⑪ 独 特　　　dútè
⑫ 享 有　　　xiǎngyǒu
⑬ 一 度　　　yídù
⑭ 支 柱　　　zhīzhù

大 萌：

四川被称为"天府之国"，气候适宜。这里土地肥沃、山水环绕，非常适合蚕桑业的发展，蚕桑业的发展就促使了纺织业的进步。四川出产的"蜀锦"品质好、数量大，成为当时皇室和达官贵人才能拥有的奢侈品，享有"母天下锦"的美誉。

两三千年前，四川人就从蚕吐丝做茧中得到启发，开始从茧里抽丝织锦，后人称这种"锦"为"蜀锦"。这期间蜀锦不断地改进工艺、增加品种、发展壮大，到汉唐时期就非常有名了。现在，蜀锦与南京云锦、苏州宋锦、广西壮锦并称为"中国四大名锦"。

蜀锦以经向彩条和彩条添花为特色，又因历史悠久和工艺独特而享有"母天下锦"的美誉，成为历史上只有皇室和达官贵人才能享有的奢侈品，并一度成为国家的主要财政来源和经济支柱。而现在的蜀锦更多是以工艺品和礼品的形式出现在大众生活里。

Wen Xiaoxi: Why is Sichuanese brocade called "Shu brocade"?

Da Meng: Because "Shu" is another name for Sichuan.

Wen Xiaoxi: In the character " 蜀 " " 虫 " is the radical for "insect". Why was this character chosen for Sichuan?

Da Meng: "Shu" is an ancient species of silkworm, or insect. The ancient king of Shu taught the Sichuanese how to plant mulberry trees and raise silkworms, which led the Sichuanese to be the first to raise domestic silkworms. Their practice became known throughout China and gave Sichuan the alternative name of "Shu".

Jiang Yihua: Why was Sichuan his place of choice for developing the mulberry and silkworm industries?

Da Meng: Sichuan is called "The Land of Plenty" , thanks to its ideal climate, fertile land, and a geographical position surrounded by mountains and water, which makes it a perfectly suitable place for silkworm breeding and mulberry growing as an industry. This industry's development also contributed to the progress of the textile industry. Sichuan-made Shu brocade was of good quality and produced in large quantities, making it a luxury product only the royal family and members of high society could afford to possess. Sichuan was reputed to be "the mother of all brocades in China".

Two or three thousand years ago, the Sichuanese drew inspiration from silkworms spinning cocoons and began to reel off raw silk from these cocoons for stitching brocades. This kind of brocade was later called "Shu brocade". During this period, the craft of Sichuan brocade was in a constant process of improvement: new products came about, and the art expanded and matured. During the Han and Tang Dynasties, Shu brocade already was incredibly famous. Today, Shu brocade, Nanjing's Yun brocade, Suzhou's Song brocade and Guangxi's Zhuang are called "China's four most famous schools of brocade".

Shu brocade, which is characterized by colorful warp stripes and vivid motifs, is renowned as "the mother of all brocades in China", owing to its long history and unique craftmanship. It became a luxury product only the royal family and members of high society could afford to enjoy and turned into one of the country's main sources of financial revenue and economic pillar. In today's society, Shu brocade has taken the role of art and gifting.

词语

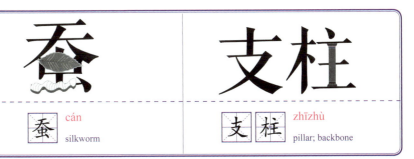

| 蚕 | cán
silkworm | 支柱 | zhīzhù
pillar; backbone |

jiǎn 茧	cocoon	qǐ fā 启 发	enlighten; stimulate
zhī jǐn 织 锦	brocade	gǎi jìn 改 进	improve; make better
gōng yì 工 艺	arts and crafts; industrial arts; craftmanship	zhuàng dà 壮 大	expand; strengthen
yōu jiǔ 悠 久	long; long-standing; age-old	dú tè 独 特	unique; distinct
xiǎng yǒu 享 有	enjoy (rights, prestige…)	yí dù 一 度	once; on one occasion; for a time

bié chēng 别 称	another name; alternative name
sāng 桑	mulberry (tree)
shì yí 适 宜	suitable; appropriate; favourable
cù shǐ 促 使	spur; promote; drive

cán-chóng lèi 蚕 虫 类	silkworm species
yáng míng tiān xià 扬 名 天 下	become world-famous; become known throughout the country
féi wò 肥 沃	(of soil, land) fertile; rich
měi yù 美 誉	good reputation; famous for sth.

专有名词

1. 天府之国 / tiānfǔ zhīguó / Land of Plenty; Land of Abundance

2. 经向彩条 / jīngxiàng cǎitiáo / colorful warp stripes

3. 彩条添花 / cǎitiáo tiānhuā / vivid motif

语言点

1. 使……成为　　2. 被称为　　3. 与……并称为

4. 因……而　　5. 以……的形式

思考

1. 中国四大名锦各自都有些什么特色？请你从网络或者别的资料查找答案。

2. "天府之国"是什么意思？你觉得四川为什么会被称为"天府之国"？

第三课 【锦官城的由来】
Lesson 3 【The Origin of the "City of the Brocade Officer"】

文小西：

你们看，书上说"晓看红湿处，花重锦官城①"，这个"锦"也是蜀锦吗？

大 萌：

是的，这是唐诗中的名句。说的就是成都的景致——有晨风，有清露，有花香……

文小西：

嗯……真美，怪不得现在很多人都说成都是一个来了就不想走的城市呢。

江一华：

"锦官城"就是成都？为什么呢？

大 萌：

那是很久很久以前的事儿啦……

① 名 句　míngjù
② 景 致　jǐngzhì
③ 晨 风　chénfēng
④ 清 露　qīnglù
⑤ 怪不得　guài bu de

① "晓看红湿处，花重锦官城"是唐朝诗人杜甫《春夜喜雨》里的一句。诗人这句诗是在想象一夜春雨之后，万物生长，花儿带雨开放，整个成都都变成了花的海洋。

①称　帝　　　chēng dì
②贸　易　　　màoyì
③财　政　　　cáizhèng
④来　源　　　láiyuán
⑤朝　廷　　　cháotíng
⑥设　置　　　shèzhì
⑦修　　　　　xiū
⑧区　域　　　qūyù
⑨如　今　　　rújīn
⑩浸　　　　　jìn
⑪五光十色　　wǔguāng shísè

　　三国时期，刘备在成都称帝。当时成都的蜀锦是对外贸易的主要商品，是国家财政收入的主要来源。因此朝廷专门设置锦官来管理蜀锦生产，并且修了一道城墙来保护蜀锦生产，这一道城墙范围以内的区域就是"锦官城"。锦官城的地址在如今的成都市百花潭公园附近。后来就以"锦城"或"锦官城"作为成都的别称。锦工织完锦后要把这些锦拿到江中洗，各种颜色的锦浸在江水中，远远看去，江水也变得五光十色，像锦一样漂亮，所以这条江得名"锦江"。锦工居住的地方就是现在的"锦里"。

Wen Xiaoxi: Look, this book says, "Come dawn, we'll see splashes of wet red – The flowers in the City of the Brocade Officer, weighed down with rain". Does "brocade" here also refer to Shu brocade?

Da Meng: It does. This is a famous verse of a Tang poem, which describes Chengdu's scenery: the morning breeze, the dew, the fragrant flowers…

Wen Xiaoxi: Yes, it's really wonderful. No wonder there are so many people saying that Chengdu is not a place you want to leave once you've arrived.

Jiang Yihua: "City of the Brocade Officer" refers to Chengdu? How come?

Da Meng: Well, that's a story from long, long ago…

During the Three Kingdoms Period, Liu Bei proclaimed himself emperor in Chengdu. At that time, Shu brocade was Chengdu's main commodity in foreign trade and the main source of national financial revenue. Therefore, the imperial court set up special officers to manage the production of Shu brocade and also erected a wall to protect the production. These officers are the namesake of the "City of the Brocade Officer". This City once was located nearby today's Baihuatan Park in Chengdu. Later on,"Brocade City" or "City of the Brocade Officer" has become Chengdu's alternative name. Brocade weavers would take the finished brocade to the river to wash it. The brocades'myriads of colors would be immersed in the water and be seen from afar, as they made the rivers bright with many colors and as beautiful as the brocade itself, which gave the river the name "Brocade River". The brocade weavers lived at a place where today's "Jinli" is located.

"Come dawn, we'll see splashes of wet red – The flowers in the City of the Brocade Officer, weighed down with rain" (translation by Brendan O'Kane, adapted) is a verse from "Spring Rain" by Tang Dynasty poet Du Fu. This verse portrays Chengdu after a night of spring rain, when everything is growing and the flowers still wet from rain are blooming, turning the whole city into an ocean of flowers.

词语

设置 	浸
设置 **shè zhì** set up; establish; install; configure (computing)	浸 **jìn** soak; immerse

míng jù 名 句	well-known phrase	jǐng zhì 景 致	view; scenery; scene
chén fēng 晨 风	morning wind	qīng lù 清 露	dew
mào yì 贸 易	trade	cái zhèng 财 政	(public) finance
lái yuán 来 源	source; origin	chēng dì 称 帝	proclaim oneself emperor
xiū 修	build; construct	qū yù 区 域	area; region; district
rú jīn 如 今	nowadays; now	wǔ guāng shí sè 五 光 十 色	bright and multicolored; dazzling

语言点

1. 怪不得　　　　2. 以……作为……

思考

1. 成都为什么被称为"锦官城"？

2. 除了锦江和锦里，你还知道哪些和"锦"有关系的成都地名？

3. 在你的国家，有没有像成都这样用一种特产来命名一座城市的？如果有，请说明。

第四课 【蜀锦织机】
Lesson 4 【The Shu Brocade Loom】

（一）

① 寸锦寸金　cùnjǐn cùnjīn
② 材料　　　cáiliào
③ 并　　　　bìng
④ 之所以　　zhī suó yǐ
⑤ 织机　　　zhījī
⑥ 织　　　　zhī

江一华：

大萌，书上说"寸锦寸金"，蜀锦真有这么贵吗？为什么会这么贵呢？

文小西：

是因为材料很难得吗？

大萌：

四川的蚕桑丝绸业起源很早，成都作为原材料产地之一，蜀锦的材料并不难得。蜀锦之所以贵，用现在的话说就是"人工贵"。

文小西：

人工贵？

大萌：

是的。两个人，一台织机，一天大概也只能织出几厘米的蜀锦……

世人大多惊叹于蜀锦的精美，却不知蜀锦的织造非常困难。一名锦工的学习至少要五年的时间，而一名优秀的锦工则需更长时间的培养。织锦前，经线纬线从原料检验到上机织造就要经过12道工序。织锦时，两名锦工相互配合，一人坐在织机上方拉经线，一人坐在织机下面织纬线，一经一纬，循环往复，重复一百多遍才能织出一厘米的蜀锦，一天下来也只能织出几厘米而已。一匹蜀锦，从图案的设计到锦缎的完成，短则四五个月，长则好几年。这就是手工织造的蜀锦一米就要上万人民币的原因。所以我们说"寸锦寸金"其实并不夸张。

① 惊 叹	jīngtàn
② 却	què
③ 织 造	zhīzào
④ 锦 工	jǐngōng
⑤ 培 养	péiyǎng
⑥ 经 线	jīngxiàn
⑦ 纬 线	wěixiàn
⑧ 检 验	jiǎnyàn
⑨ 工 序	gōngxù
⑩ 循 环	xúnhuán
⑪ 锦 缎	jǐnduàn

（二）

文小西：
原来织造蜀锦这么复杂啊。

江一华：
是啊。我对蜀锦织机的样子非常好奇。

大萌：
蜀锦的织机叫"花楼织机"，四川省博物馆就有一台，长6米，宽1.5米，高5米。

文小西：
真大！

江一华：
所有的织机都这样吗？这么大会不会不方便？

① 花楼织机	huālóu zhījī
② 功 能	gōngnéng
③ 踞织机	jùzhījī
④ 腰 机	yāo jī
⑤ 斜织机	xié zhī jī
⑥ 束综织机	shùzōng zhījī
⑦ 花绫织机	huālíng zhījī
⑧ 操 作	cāozuò
⑨ 效 率	xiàolǜ
⑩ 零 件	língjiàn
⑪ 竹 扣	zhúkòu
⑫ 丝丝入扣	sīsī rùkòu
⑫ 亲眼目睹	qīnyǎn mùdǔ
⑬ 出 土	chūtǔ

⑭提花织机　　tíhuā zhījī
⑮模　型　　　móxíng
⑯印　证　　　yìnzhèng
⑰湮　没　　　yānmò

大萌：

蜀锦经过了两三千年的发展，它的织机在大小、功能等方面都不断地改进，先后经历了踞织机、腰机、斜织机、束综织机、花绫织机，最后才发展到花楼织机。花楼织机不太常见，比较大，操作的时候必须两人配合，不过花楼织机的效率和织出来的锦都是最好的。

　　花楼蜀锦织机源于三国时期。每一台织机都是由一千多个零件构成——由9 980多根蚕线组成的经线部分和由980多个很小的竹扣组合而成的纬线部分。成语"丝丝入扣"就是从这儿来的。

　　然而，当时蜀锦的美、蜀地纺织业的发达，我们都无法亲眼目睹，无法验证这是传说还是真实。直到2012年夏天，成都市出土了汉代提花织机模型，这才印证了成都就是历史上丝绸之路南起点的说法。

　　经过了千年的岁月，大多数蜀锦织机都已经湮没在历史中，或损坏，或遗失。还能使用的织机目前仅存三台，分别放在成都蜀江锦院、四川博物院和北京的故宫博物院。

Part 1

Jiang Yihua: Da Meng, this book says, "an inch of brocade, one inch of gold". Is Shu brocade really that expensive?

Wen Xiaoxi: Is it because the material is so hard to get by?

Da Meng: Sichuan's sericulture industry was started very early on. As Chengdu is one of the original producers of the raw materials, they are, in fact, not rare. Shu brocade's exorbitant price is due to high labor cost, as we would say today.

Wen Xiaoxi: High labor cost?

Da Meng: Correct. Two people, one loom, they may only be able to produce a few centimeters' worth of Shu brocade to per day…

Many people from all over the world marvel at the exquisite Shu brocade, but they do not know how difficult weaving this brocade is. A brocade weaver has to study at least five years and an outstanding weaver needs even more training. When weaving brocades, it takes 12 processes to make warps and wefts, starting with examining the raw material and ending with weaving on the loom. During weaving, two weavers complement in each other: one sits on the loom and pulls the warps, while the other is under the loom and weaves the wefts, and so it goes on, warp for weft, weft for warp. Only one centimeter's worth of brocade is produced after more than 100 cycles of this seemingly unending process; at the end of a working day, the weavers merely produce several centimeters' worth of brocade. A single piece of Shu brocade, from designing the motif to the finished product, takes four to five months at the least, and several years at the most. This is the reason why one meter of hand-woven Shu brocade costs tens of thousands RMB. Saying, "one inch of brocade, one inch of gold" is indeed no exaggeration.

Part 2

Wen Xiaoxi: Who would've thought that weaving Shu brocade is that complicated!

Jiang Yihua: I know, right? I'm actually very curious now what a Shu brocade loom looks like!

Da Meng: These looms are called "Hualou Looms". You can see one in the Sichuan Museum: it is 6 meters long, 1.5 meters wide and 5 meters high.

Wen Xiaoxi: Talk about big! It's even bigger than our classroom!

Jiang Yihua: Are all looms like this? If they are that big, aren't they kind of inconvenient?

Da Meng: Shu brocade has a history of two to three thousand years. The dimensions, features and so on of these looms were constantly being improved upon, and they went from squat looms to waist looms, oblique looms, beam-weaving looms, Hualing looms and finally Hualou looms. Hualou looms are a rare sight. They are quite big, so two people working together are needed for operation. But this loom's efficiency and woven brocades are the best.

Hualou looms were created during the Three Kingdoms period. Every loom was built out of more than 1,000 components, the warps consisted of more than 9,980 silk threads and the wefts of more than 980 small bamboo buttons. The saying"All the silk yarns go through the buttons" has its origins from here.

However, the beauty of Shu brocade and the flourishing textile industry of the former state of Shu was not something we could witness with our own eyes, and we were not able to say for certain whether this era was only the stuff of legends or whether it really happened. That is, until the summer of 2012, when a Tihua loom model dating from the Han dynasty was unearthed in Chengdu, confirming that Chengdu was indeed the historical starting point of the Southern Silk Road.

Through one thousand years of history, most of the Brocade looms fell either into oblivion, were damaged or lost. At present, there are only three looms that still can be used, which are respectively placed in Shujiang Jinyuan, in the Sichuan Provincial Museum and the National Palace Museum in Beijing.

词 语

织 机	循 环
zhījī loom	xúnhuán circle; loop

cùn jǐn cùn jīn 寸 锦 寸 金	one inch of brocade, one inch of gold	cái liào 材 料	material
bìng bú 并 不	not at all	zhī suó yǐ 之 所 以	the reason why
jīng tàn 惊 叹	wonder at; marvel at	què 却	but; yet; however
zhī zào 织 造	weave; weaving; manufacture by weaving	jǐn gōng 锦 工	brocade weaver
péi yǎng 培 养	education; training	jiǎn yàn 检 验	inspect; examine; test

gōng xù 工 序	process; work procedure
cāo zuò 操 作	operation
líng jiàn 零 件	part
sī sī rù kòu 丝 丝 入 扣	all threads neatly tied up
chū tǔ 出 土	be unearthed
yìn zhèng 印 证	confirm

gōng néng 功 能	function
xiào lǜ 效 率	efficiency
zhú kòu 竹 扣	bamboo buckle
qīn yǎn mù dǔ 亲 眼 目 睹	witness
mó xíng 模 型	model
yān mò 湮 没	annihilation

专有名词

1. 织机　　　　/ zhījī / loom

2. 经线　　　　/ jīngxiàn / warp yarn

3. 纬线　　　　/ wěixiàn / weft yarn

4. 锦缎　　　　/ jǐnduàn / brocade

5. 花楼织机　　/ Huālóu Zhījī / Hualou loom

6. 踞织机　　　/ Jù Zhījī / squat loom

7. 腰机　　　　/ Yāo Jī / waist loom

8. 斜织机　　　/ Xié Zhījī / oblique loom

9. 束综织机　　/ Shùzōng Zhījī / beam-weaving loom

10. 花绫织机　　/ Huālíng Zhījī / Hualing loom

11. 提花织机　　/ Tíhuā Zhījī / Tihua loom, Jacquard loom

12. 彩条添花　　/ cǎitiáo tiānhuā / vivid motif

语言点

1. 短则……长则   2. 或……或

思 考

1. "寸锦寸金"是什么意思？为什么蜀锦"寸锦寸金"？

2. 蜀锦织机一共经历了几种变化？这些蜀锦织机的特点是什么？

3. "丝丝入扣"跟织锦有什么关系？除此之外，你还知道哪些跟织锦有关的成语？

第五课
Lesson 5
【蜀锦的历史】
【The History of Shu Brocade】

① 西 周　Xī Zhōu
② 据　　jù
③ 记 载　jìzǎi
④ 珍 品　zhēnpǐn
⑤ 辉 煌　huīhuáng

江一华：
　　大萌，蜀锦到底是什么时候出现的？

大 萌：
　　有人认为蜀锦最早出现在西周（约公元前11 世纪—前 771 年），现在已经有两三千年了。商人们经过"南方丝绸之路"把蜀锦卖到了印度、中亚等地方。

文小西：
　　那里的人也很喜欢蜀锦吗？

大 萌：
　　据史书记载，当这些有着精美花纹的蜀锦到达公元前的罗马帝国时，受到当地人的热烈欢迎，蜀锦被认为是珍品，他们甚至称中国为"东方丝国"。

大 萌：
　　真是辉煌的时代啊！

大 萌：

蜀锦最辉煌的时期应该是在唐朝。那时候的蜀锦，不管是生产规模还是技术，都达到了顶峰，出现了很多精品。比如说《兰亭序》文字锦被作为珍品藏入宫中；安乐公主结婚定做的"单丝碧罗笼裙"用细如发丝的金线织成花鸟，更是天下绝品。

⑥唐　朝　　Tángcháo
⑦顶　峰　　dǐngfēng
⑧兰亭序　　Lántíng Xù
⑨细如发丝　xìrú fàsī
⑩锦　坊　　jǐnfáng
⑪花　样　　huāyàng

江一华：

后来呢？

大 萌：

到了明朝末年，蜀锦的恶梦也开始了。当时整个成都都被战争毁了，蜀锦的锦坊和花样也被毁了。这场恶梦持续了一两百年，直到19世纪，蜀锦才开始慢慢恢复。

Jiang Yihua: Da Meng, when did Shu brocade make its appearance?

Da Meng: Some think that the first Shu brocades emerged during the Western Zhou Dynasty (from the 11th century BC until 771 BC) and has existed for two to three thousand years now. Merchants sold Shu brocade to places such as India and Central Asia through the Southern Silk Road.

Wen Xiaoxi: The people over there also like Shu brocade?

Da Meng: According to historical records, when Shu brocade and its exquisite patterns arrived in the Roman Empire before the birth of Christ, it was well-received by the Romans: they considered Shu brocade as treasure and even called China the "Eastern Silk Country".

Wen Xiaoxi: Truly a glorious time for Shu brocade!

Da Meng: Its most glorious time was probably during the Tang Dynasty. During that time, be it scale of production or technology, the Shu brocade industry was at its peak and there were lots of brocades of fine quality. Brocade embroidered with characters of "Lanting Xu", for example, was described as treasure stored in palaces. In Princess Anle's custom-made wedding dress, a "jade-green gauze skirt made of a single yarn of silk", a gold thread as thin as hair was woven to create a pattern of flowers and birds, which turned this already priceless work of art into a gem that was second to none in the whole of China.

Jiang Yihua: And afterwards?

Da Meng: With the arrival of the late Ming Dynasty, Shu brocade was met with a terrible fate: At that time, the entirety of Chengdu was destroyed by a war, and so were the Shu brocade workshops and designs. This dreadful period lasted for one to two hundred years until the 19th century, when the Shu brocade industry began to slowly recover.

词 语

记载	顶峰
记 载 jìzǎi record; account	顶 峰 dǐngfēng peak; summit; high point; pinnacle

jù 据	according to; on the grounds of	xì rú fà sī 细 如 发 丝	as thin as hair
huī huáng 辉 煌	brilliant; splendid; glorious	jǐn fáng 锦 坊	brocade workshop
zhēn pǐn 珍 品	treasure; valuable object; curio	huā yàng 花 样	decorative pattern; design

专 有 名 词

1. 西周   / Xī Zhōu / West Zhou Dynasty

2. 唐朝   / Tángcháo / the Tang Dynasty

3. 兰亭序   / Lántíng Xù / the Lanting Xu; literally: "Preface to the Poems Collected from the Orchid Pavilion"; a piece of Chinese calligraphy work considered to be written by Wang Xizhi from the East Jin Dynasty (317 – 420)

语言点

不管是……还是……

思考

1. 中国为什么被古罗马人称为"东方丝国"？
2. 请你简单介绍一下蜀锦的历史。

第六课 【蜀锦的品种】
Lesson 6 【The Shu Brocade Products】

蜀锦的花样有很多，我们根据这些花样的图案和色彩，把蜀锦分成了很多不同的品种：月华锦、雨丝锦、浣花锦、方方锦、现代蜀锦等。

（一）月华锦

月华锦非常精美，但是也非常复杂，一匹月华锦光经线就要14272根。在织造的时候，锦工们需要把各种颜色的彩丝按照颜色的深浅排列，由浅入深，又由深入浅，看起来就像月光再现在锦上一样，月华锦的设计灵感大概就来自于美丽朦胧的月光吧。

（二）雨丝锦

雨丝锦的特点就是把白经（白色经线）和色经（彩色经线）按比例排列，白经由少变多，色经由多变少，形成色白相间的效果，就像天空的"彩雨"。在这些"彩雨"里面再织上各种图案。雨丝锦和月华锦的区别就是雨丝锦颜色的深浅过度是通过白经和色经的宽窄来实现的，色白对比清晰；而月华锦颜色的深浅过渡是朦胧的、是逐渐变化的。

（三）浣花锦

浣花锦又称"花锦"，源于宋代。浣花锦的纹样极为丰富，看起来古朴、典雅又大方。传说是长期在浣花溪上洗锦的锦女们，根据落花流水的波纹设计的。一般以梅花、桃花为题材，散落的花瓣漂浮在水纹上，花随水流，情趣深厚。

① 匹　　　　pǐ
② 光　　　　guāng
③ 按照……排列　ànzhào …páiliè
④ 由……入　yóu… rù
⑤ 灵 感　　línggǎn
⑥ 朦 胧　　ménglóng
⑦ 相 间　　xiāngjiàn
⑧ 过 度　　guòdù
⑨ 宽 窄　　kuānzhǎi
⑩ 实 现　　shíxiàn
⑪ 清 晰　　qīngxī

⑫ 宋 代　　SòngDài
⑬ 古 朴　　gǔpǔ
⑭ 典 雅　　diǎnyǎ
⑮ 大 方　　dàfāng
⑯ 波 纹　　bōwén
⑰ 设 计　　shèjì
⑱ 漂 浮　　piāofú
⑲ 情 趣　　qíngqù
⑳ 深 厚　　shēnhòu

㉑战 国　Zhàn Guó
㉒漫 长　màncháng
㉓创 新　chuàngxīn
㉔旺 盛　wàngshèng
㉕方 格　fānggé
㉖灵 活　línghuó
㉗呈 现　chéngxiàn
㉘严 谨　yánjǐn
㉙灵 动　língdòng
㉚限 于　xiànyú
㉛高 档　gāodàng
㉜精 细　jīngxì

（四）方方锦

　　方方锦起源于战国时期，在漫长的历史中不断创新，保持着旺盛的生命力。20 世纪五六十年代，方方锦曾被选做中国领导人出国访问的国家级礼品。

　　方方锦的特点是色经和彩经交织成方格，在方格里再织上各种图案。梅兰竹菊、石榴莲花等都可以织在方方锦里。方方锦的方格很整齐，方格内图案灵活多变，整体呈现出一种严谨与灵动结合的艺术美。

（五）现代蜀锦

　　随着旅游业的发展以及人们物质生活水平的不断提高，人们对蜀锦产品的需求发生了很大的变化。蜀锦也不仅限于衣物，旅游纪念品、礼品、室内高档用品的需求也很大。现代蜀锦要求产品颜色鲜艳，图案有特色，强调制作精细，如"百子图"锦、"天府"锦、熊猫系列等。

Shu brocade has a lot of designs. Based on the pattern and the color of these designs, we can divide Shu brocade into many different varieties: moonlight brocade, raindrop brocade, fallen flower and flowing river brocade, check-patterned brocade, modern brocade, and so on.

1.Moonlight Brocade

Moonlight brocade is incredibly elegant, but also incredibly complex. A single roll of moonlight brocade needs 14,272 warp threads alone. During weaving, the weavers need to arrange the differently colored silk threads according to their shades, from light shades into dark shades and from dark shades into light shades, making it seem as if moonlight were sprinkled on the brocade. It was probably beautiful, hazy moonlight that inspired moonlight brocade's design.

2.Raindrop Brocade

What is so special about Raindrop brocade is the fact that the white warp yarns and colored warp yarns are arranged in a certain ratio: less white means more color and more white less color, color alternating with white, creating an effect just like "colorful rain" falling from the heavens. Various motifs are woven into this colorful rain. Raindrop and moonlight brocades differ insofar as the shade transitions of the colors in raindrop brocade are implemented through the varying width of the white and colored warp yarns, and there is a clear contrast between white and color.

Shade transitions in moonlight brocade, on the other hand, are hazy, meaning they are realized through gradual change in color.

3.Fallen Flower and Flowing River Brocade

Fallen Flower and Flowing River Brocade came about during the Song Dynasty. Its many different patterns look simple, elegant and tasteful. According to legend, it was the women who washed brocades in Huanhuaxi for a long time that came up with the design, inspired by the ripples of flowing water. Plum or peach are usually the theme; the pattern depicts scattered petals floating on water, as the petals flow with the water. Gazing at this brocade is a real delight.

4.Check-Patterned Brocade

Check-patterned brocade came about during the Warring States Period. It was continuously innovated upon in its long history and never lost its splendor. In the 1950s and 1960s, check-patterned brocades were given out as gifts by Chinese politicians during their visits abroad.

Check-patterned brocade's prominent feature is the pattern of squares that is formed by interweaving white and colored warp yarns, with patterns woven into these squares, such as plum blossoms, orchids, chrysanthemums, bamboo as well as lotus and pomegranates. The squares are neatly arranged and the patterns inside them are flexible and varied. The overall impression is one of art both precise and agile.

5.Modern Brocade

With the rise of tourism and the continuous improvement of people's material standard of living, demand for products has undergone great changes. Shu brocade is not merely limited to clothing, souvenirs and gifts demand for Shu brocade as high-quality household items is growing. Modern brocade features bright colors and distinctive patterns, with emphasis on elegance, such as Baizitu brocades, Chengdu brocades, panda brocades and so on.

词语

朦胧	设计
朦胧 ménglóng (of moonlight) dim; hazy	设计 shèjì design

pǐ 匹	measure word for rolls of cloth or silk	guāng 光	only; alone
àn ... pái liè 按……排列	according to...arrange/ align/put in order	yóu ... rù 由……入	from...into
líng gǎn 灵 感	inspiration (for creative work)	xiāng jiàn 相 间	alternate with; intersperse with
guò dù 过 度	transition; transitioning	kuān zhǎi 宽 窄	width
qīng xī 清 晰	clear; distinct	gǔ pǔ 古 朴	(of art...) simple and unsophisticated

dà fāng 大 方	generous; natural and poised
piāo fú 漂 浮	float
shēn hòu 深 厚	deep
màn cháng 漫 长	very long
wàng shèng 旺 盛	vigorous; exuberant
líng huó 灵 活	flexible
yán jǐn 严 谨	rigorous; strict; precise
xiàn yú 限 于	confined to; limited to

diǎn yǎ 典 雅	(of decoration…) refined; elegant
bō wén 波 纹	ripple
qíng qù 情 趣	delight; appeal
chuàng xīn 创 新	innovate
fāng gé 方 格	pattern of squares; checked pattern
chéng xiàn 呈 现	present (a certain appearance)
líng dòng 灵 动	nimble; agile
gāo dàng 高 档	superior quality; high grade; top grade

shí xiàn 实 现	implement; realize

jīng xì 精 细	fine; meticulous; careful

专有名词

1. 宋代　/ Sòng Dài / Song Dynasty

2. 战国　/ Zhàn Guó / Warring States Period

思考

1. 请简单介绍一下文中提到的五种蜀锦。

2. 除了这五种蜀锦，你还知道哪些蜀锦品种？请查找资料，跟同学介绍并讨论。

Lesson 7 【寓合纹】

【Symbolic Motifs】

① 讲 究　　*jiǎngjiū*
② 寓合纹　　*Yù Hé Wén*
③ 鹤　　　　*hè*
④ 寓 意　　*yùyì*

文小西:

蜀锦上的图案，有的是花，有的是动物，它们有什么讲究吗？

大 萌:

当然有。每一个图都有特别的意义，把它们组合在一起可以表达祝福、吉祥等美好的意义，这就叫作"寓合纹"。

江一华:

比如，在中国文化里，龙代表皇上，凤代表皇后，龙凤表示吉祥。

大 萌:

对，还有龟和鹤表示长寿，牡丹花表示富贵。

文小西:

为什么四川人这么喜欢有寓意的东西？为什么图案一定要有这些特别的寓意呢？它们有什么讲究吗？

大 萌：

我想这跟文化有关系吧，我们都希望自己的生活越来越好，所以用各种方式来表达对吉祥平安的追求，体现在蜀锦上就是每个图案都有意思，每个意思都和吉祥有关系。这寄托了四川人民对美好生活的向往。

⑤寄　托　　jìtuō
⑥向　往　　xiàngwǎng

　　在蜀锦艺人手里，各种神话传说、历史故事以及动物、植物等等都可以组合成有意义的图案，这就是"寓合纹"。它含有吉祥、如意、顺利、喜庆等美好吉利的寓意。最有代表性的就是"五星出东方利中国"织锦护膊，它属于国家一级文物，长18.5厘米，宽12.5厘米。它由9 000根经线织成，用青红黄白绿五组色经织出星云、鸟兽和代表日月的红白圆纹样，上下花纹之间还有"五星出东方利中国"几个字。这个织锦护膊的织造工艺非常复杂，是汉式织锦最高技术的代表。

⑦神话传说
　shénhuà chuánshuō
⑧组　合　　zǔhé
⑨护　膊　　hùbó

Wen Xiaoxi: Some of the motifs on Shu brocade are flowers; others are animals. Is there more to them?

Da Meng: Of course there is. Each motif has its own special meaning. By putting them together, they can express, for example, blessings and auspiciousness. These are called "symbolic motifs".

Jiang Yihua: For example, in Chinese culture, the dragon represents the emperor, while the phoenix represents the empress, so the dragon and the phoenix together express auspiciousness.

Da Meng: Exactly. Other examples include the turtle and the crane that express longevity, and peony flowers that stand for wealth.

Wen Xiaoxi: How come the Sichuanese like these implied meanings so much? Why does there have to be a special meaning attached to these motifs?

Da Meng: I think there's a cultural reason for that. The Sichuanese have been deeply influenced by Daoist culture and often express their aspirations for auspiciousness and peace through various ways, which can also be seen on Shu brocade. Every motif has a meaning and every meaning is related to auspiciousness. In this way, the Sichuanese give expression to their expectations of a happy life.

In the hands of Shu brocade artists, any animals, plants or other objects of mythology, legend, history or stories may be combined in a motif to convey meaning. This is what "symbolic motifs" are all about. These brocades all imply auspiciousness, satisfaction, success, jubilation or other propitious meanings. The most representative example is the "Five stars rise in the East, benefitting China" brocade armband, which belongs to China's first-grade cultural objects. It is 18.5 cm long and 12.5 cm wide. It consists of 9,000 warps: five groups of colors – blue, red, yellow, white and green – are woven into clouds, stars, birds and other animals, while red and white rounded patterns represent the sun and the moon. Top and bottom, between the motifs, are embroided with the words "Five stars rising in the East benefiting China". The craftsmanship of this brocade armband is highly complex and represents the pinnacle of weaving that was reached during the Han Dynasty.

词语

鹤	向往	组合
鹤 hè crane	向往 xiàngwǎng yearn for; look forward to	组合 zǔhé combine; make up; compose; constitute

jiǎng jiū 讲究	pay attention to; sth requiring careful study; art	jì tuō 寄托	a thing in which you invest (hope, energy…); find sustenance in; entrust to the care of; give expression to
yù yì 寓意	implied meaning; message	Yù Hé Wén 寓合纹	symbolic motif
shén huà chuán shuō 神话传说	myths and legends	hù bó 护膊	armband

思考

1. "寓合纹"是什么？

2. 中国文化里，还有些什么美好寓意的形象？

3. 在你们国家的文化里，哪些形象有美好的寓意？请简单介绍一下。

第八课【蜀绣】
Lesson 8 【 Shu Embroidery 】

①难不倒　nán bù dǎo
②聪　慧　cōnghuì
③绣　种　xiùzhǒng

文小西：

蜀锦精美而昂贵，普通百姓买不起，怎么办呢？

大　萌：

这难不倒聪慧的四川人民。他们在普通的衣服上，用彩色的丝线绣出各种漂亮的图案。我们叫它"蜀绣"。

江一华：

蜀绣的历史也很悠久吗？

大　萌：

对，蜀绣是中国最古老的绣种之一。《华阳国志》记载，汉代以前人们衣服上的图案都是画上去的，只有四川的蜀绣是针线绣上去的。

中国人喜爱丝织品，从古至今，人们都喜欢在丝织品上织绣美丽的图案。"蜀绣"就是四川成都地区生产的绣品。蜀绣非常精美，它可以是用来观赏的艺术品，也可以是很实用的生活用品。蜀绣最盛行的时候，几乎是"家家女红，户户针工"。浪漫的四川人总能在平淡的生活里找到美好。因为刺绣，生活变得很精彩，生活用品里大到窗帘，小到钱包，随处可见刺绣。古代女子平日最主要的工作就是刺绣——绣家里的生活用品，绣自己的手帕，最主要的是绣自己的嫁衣，有时候还偷偷地绣一个荷包送给喜欢的人。

① 丝织品　　sīzhīpǐn
② 从古至今　cónggǔ zhìjīn
③ 观　赏　　guānshǎng
④ 实　用　　shíyòng
⑤ 盛　行　　shèngxíng
⑥ 家家女红，户户针工
　　jiājiānǚgōng, hùhùzhēngōng
⑦ 平　淡　　píngdàn
⑧ 荷　包　　hébāo

Wen Xiaoxi: Shu brocade was both elegant and expensive, so ordinary people wouldn't be able to afford it. What were they going to do about that?

Da Meng: That did not pose a problem for the bright Sichuanese working people. Using colored silk threads, they embroidered beautiful motifs into ordinary clothing. This is what we call "Sichuan embroidery".

Jiang Yihua: Shu embroidery has a long history, right?

Da Meng: Right. Sichuan embroidery is one of China's oldest embroideries. As is recorded in the Chronicles of Huayang, people before the Han Dynasty would draw motifs onto their clothes, while only Shu embroidery was stitched onto clothing.

Chinese people love silk fabrics. From ancient times until today, the people have enjoyed embroidering beautiful motifs onto silk. "Shu embroidery" refers to embroidery products in Chengdu, Sichuan. Shu embroidery is incredibly elegant. It can be admired as a piece of art, but can also be used as an article for daily use. When Shu embroidery was at its most popular, almost "every household had a woman stitching". The romantic Sichuanese always found something beautiful even in the dullest moments of life, because thanks to embroidery, life became wonderful, and as an article for daily use, embroidery could be found everywhere at any time, on something as big as curtains, and also on something as small as wallets. In ancient times, women's daily main work was stitching embroideries on articles of daily use: on their own handkerchiefs and, most importantly, on their own wedding dresses. Sometimes they would also secretly embroider small pouches for somebody they were fond of.

词语

 sī zhī pǐn silk fabrics; item made from woven silk	guān shǎng look at sth with pleasure; view and admire; watch (sth marvelous)	hé bāo small bag (for carrying money and odds and ends); pouch

nán bù dǎo 难 不 倒	not to pose a problem for sb; cannot stump sb;	cōng huì 聪 慧	bright; witty; intelligent
xiù zhǒng 绣 种	(variety of)embroidery	cóng gǔ zhì jīn 从 古 至 今	from past to present
shí yòng 实 用	practical use; practical	shèng xíng 盛 行	be popular; be in vogue; be prevalent
jiā jiā nǚ gōng 家 家 女 红 hù hù zhēn gōng 户 户 针 工	literarily: every family has a woman needleworker, every household has needlework; every household has a woman stitching	píng dàn 平 淡	dull; ordinary; nothing special

语言点

1. 可以是……也可以是……　　2. 大到……小到……

思考

1. 蜀绣和蜀锦有什么不一样？

2. 你们国家有刺绣吗？你们一般会绣什么东西？

3. "家家女红，户户针工"是什么意思？蜀绣为什么会这么流行？

第九课
Lesson 9 【蜀绣针法】
【Shu Embroidery Stitches】

　　如果说蜀锦是从织机里织出来的艺术品，那么蜀绣就是从针尖上绣出来的艺术品。中国的四大名绣（苏绣、粤绣、蜀绣、湘绣）针法和风格都各自不同，其中针法最丰富多变的就是蜀绣——有十二个大类、一百多种。

　　在蜀绣的这么多针法里，最特别的就是"晕针"，它主要用来表现色彩的浓淡变化，因为有中国画的晕染效果，所以叫"晕针"。"晕针"的针法分为三三针、二二针、二三针三种，三种针法起针的时候都要求很整齐，区别就是针脚的长短排列不一样。

　　绣的内容不同，就要求用不同的针法。比如"晕针"常常用来绣鸟兽的羽毛或者尾巴。如果需要绣一些弯曲的线条，比如头发、胡须、人物的衣褶、烟云、树藤等，可以用"滚针"。在金鱼的尾部或者鸟雀的羽毛尖处，添加色彩的时候用"撒针"。绣人的眉眼的时候，常常用"盖针"，用一个色块盖住另外一个色块。在绣鸟的脚或者竹节的时候，需要有凹凸的感觉，就用"扎针"。

①晕　染　　yùnrǎn
②针　脚　　zhēnjiǎo
③起　针　　qǐzhēn
④弯　曲　　wānqū
⑤胡　须　　húxū
⑥衣　褶　　yīzhě
⑦树　藤　　shùténg
⑧凹　凸　　āotū
⑨如果说……，那么……
　　rú guǒ shuō …，nà me …

If Shu brocade is art woven from a loom, then Shu embroidery is art stitched from the point of a needle. China's four big schools of embroidery (Su, Yue, Shu and Xiang) differ in their stitches and styles, with Shu embroidery being the most rich and varied: 122 needlework techniques divided into 12 big categories.

Among the many Shu embroidery stitches, the most special is the yun stitch, which is mainly used to express shades of color. Its name is derived from the shading effect it gives to the embroidery, just like Chinese paintings. The yun stitch can be divided into three stitches: the full 3 stitch, the 2 and 2 stitch, and the 2 and 3 stitch. All three of them look neat and tidy; their difference lies in the length and arrangement of the stitches.

As there are many themes to embroidery, there also many different stitches to be used. For example, the yun stitch is often used for wings or tails of birds and other animals. The gun stitch is used if a curved line is to be stitched, for example, hair, beards, folds in clothing, smoke, mists, clouds, tree vines and so on. The sa stitch is used for goldfish tails or the tips of bird feathers or for adding color. The gai stitch is often used for stitching human eyebrows where one color lump covers another. The zha stitch is used for bird feet or bamboo, which require the embroidery to feel bumpy.

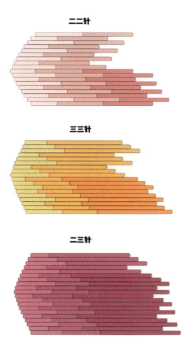

词语

针 脚	弯 曲

	zhēnjiǎo			wānqū
针 脚	stitch		弯 曲	bend; curve

yùn rǎn 晕 染	shading (wash painting technique); smudge
hú xū 胡 须	beard
shù téng 树 藤	tree vine

qǐ zhēn 起 针	to stitch (action)
yī zhě 衣 褶	fold (in clothing)
āo tū 凹 凸	uneven; bumpy

语言点

如果说……，那么……

思考

1. 请简单介绍一下中国四大名绣各自的特点和区别。

2. 你们国家的刺绣针法复杂吗？请介绍一两种特别的针法。

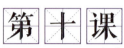

Lesson 10 【双面绣】
【Double-Sided Embroidery】

蜀绣在几千年的发展历史里，经过了从民间到皇室、从简单到精细的发展过程。从最早的单面绣，到后来的双面绣，再后来出现了更精细的异色绣和三异绣等很多种类。

单面绣是最普通的蜀绣品种，它只要求正面的针脚平整，比较简单，刺绣初学者一般比较喜欢。双面绣也比较常见，但是它要求正反两面的图案一样，两面的针脚都要很平整，所以有一点儿难度。异色秀的难度比双面绣更大一点儿。异色秀的正反两面图案一样，但是一部分的颜色不太一样。蜀绣里最难的就是三异绣。三异绣正反两面图案、颜色、针法都不一样。三异绣对刺绣的手艺要求非常高，两面各不一样，但是都很整齐漂亮，看不到针脚。

双面绣、异色秀和三异绣都要求画工先在蜀锦上画好图案，绣工再根据图案配色、刺绣。

① 作 为　　zuòwéi
② 标 志　　biāozhì
③ 入门级　　rùménjí
④ 针 脚　　zhēnjiǎo
⑤ 非物质文化遗产
　　fēi wùzhì wénhuà yíchǎn
⑥ 座 屏　　zuòpíng
⑦ 缎 底　　duàndǐ
⑧ 水 纹　　shuǐwén
⑨ 正 反　　zhèngfǎn
⑩ 虚 实　　xūshí
⑪ 色 阶　　sèjiē
⑫ 浸 针　　jìnzhēn
⑬ 截 针　　jiézhēn
⑭ 沙 针　　shāzhēn

（一）

文小西：
原来蜀绣一点也不简单。

江一华：
古代女子真厉害！

大萌：
作为中国四大名绣之一、中国国家级非物质文化遗产、中国地理标志保护产品，蜀绣怎么可能简单呢？不过前面说的都是些入门级的针法，你们再来看看这个……

江一华：
"芙蓉锦鲤"？看起来没有特别的地方啊。

大萌：
看看它的背面。

文小西：
为什么它背面也有一样的图案？

大 萌:

这就是"双面绣"。在一块布上，同时绣出正反色彩一样的图案。一般的绣法只要求正面整齐漂亮，背面的针脚不用管；而双面绣则要求正反两面一样整齐美观。

"芙蓉锦鲤"是一座双面绣大座屏，长4.4米、高2.5米，浅米黄色的缎底上绣了32条不同大小、不同样子的红黑鲤鱼和一些漂亮的芙蓉花，屏上没绣一丝水纹，却让人觉得看到的都是水。这座屏风采用了晕针、浸针、截针、沙针等几十种不同的针法。为表现鱼的远近虚实，以及不同的光线，使用不同色阶的同色丝线就有18种。

（二）

文 小西:

18种不同色阶的同色丝线？什么意思？

大 萌:

比如说，绿色包括深深浅浅的不同的18种绿。

文 小西:

好复杂！

①蜀宫夜宴　Shǔgōng Yèyàn
②细　心　　xìxīn
③耐　心　　nàixīn
④不仅……也　bù jǐn …yě

大 萌：

确实非常麻烦。不过这样才能保证图案的精美。你们再来看看这幅现代的"蜀宫夜宴图"，高 1.1 米，宽 2 米，它是 5 个人用了 3 年多的时间才完成的。所以，一幅蜀绣的完成，不仅需要细心，也需要耐心。

江一华：

时间就是金钱。所以，手工的蜀绣也非常昂贵吗？

大 萌：

当然。

In its history of several thousand years, Shu embroidery has undergone a long development process, from ordinary homes to palaces, from simple to sophisticated; from the earliest single-sided embroidery, to the later double-sided embroidery and to the many varieties that appeared much later on, such as delicate, two-color embroidery and trifecta embroidery.

Single-sided embroidery is the most common form of Shu embroidery. It only requires the stitches on the front side to be smooth and is a rather simple embroidery, usually liked by beginners of embroidery stitching. Double-sided embroidery is relatively common, but requires the motif on the front and the back to be the same and requires the stitches on both sides to be smooth. As a result, stitching this kind of embroidery is a bit more difficult. The motif of two-color embroideries is the same on both the front and the back, but certain colored parts differ. The most difficult Shu embroidery to stitch is the trifecta embroidery: the motifs, colors and stitches on both the front and the back are all completely different. Trifecta embroidery requires extremely high expertise. While both sides are different from each other, they are neat and beautiful, without any stitches to be seen.

Double-sided embroidery, two-color embroidery and trifecta embroidery require an artisan-painter to first paint a motif on the Shu brocade. Then, according to this motif, an embroidery worker matches colors and stitches the embroidery.

Part 1

Wen Xiaoxi: Who would've thought that Shu embroidery is that complicated...

Jiang Yihua: Those women back then were really something else!

Da Meng: As one of China's four famous embroidery schools, as part of China's intangible cultural heritage, as a product of China's protection of geographical indication, why would Shu embroidery not be complicated? Having said that, what I told you before are entry-level stitches, just have a look at this...

Jiang Yihua: "Hibiscus and Koi" ? Doesn't look special to me.

Da Meng: Have a look at its back.

Wen Xiaoxi: How come the motif on the back is identical?

Da Meng: This is known as "double-sided embroidery": two identically colored motifs stitched on both the front and the back of one piece of fabric. Ordinary techniques only require the front to look neat and beautiful with little regard to the stitches on the back. Double-sided embroidery, on the other hand, is about making both front and back equally tidy and pleasing to the eye.

"Hibiscus and Koi" is double-sided embroidery stitched on a big screen placed on top of a pedestal; it is 4.4 meters long and 2.5 meters high. 32 red and black koi fish in various sizes and appearances together with some stunning hibiscus flowers are stitched on a light-beige colored satin background. There is no water pattern stitched on the screen, but the onlooker still gets the impression that they are looking at water. Dozens of different stitches were used to bring out the splendor of this embroidery, including Yun, Jin, Jie and Sha stitches. 18 various shades of the same colored silk thread were used in order to convey the perception of distance between the fish as well as differing lighting.

Part 2

Wen Xiaoxi: 18 various shades of the same colored silk thread? What's that supposed to mean?

Da Meng: For example, 18 darker and lighter shades of green.

Wen Xiaoxi: Talk about complicated!

Da Meng: It is indeed incredibly tricky, but this is what makes the motif so elegant. Have a look at this modern piece called "Banquet at Shu Palace". It is 1.1 meters tall and 2 meters wide. It took five people over three years to complete. As you can see, a piece of Shu embroidery not only needs a lot of care, but also lots of patience.

Jiang Yihua: Time is money, so is handmade Shu embroidery also extremely expensive?

Da Meng: Of course.

词语

水 纹 shuǐwén water pattern; ripples	正 反 zhèngfǎn front and back

zuò wéi 作 为	as (in the capacity of)		rù mén jí 入 门 级	entry-level; basic
biāo zhì 标 志	indication		zuò píng 座 屏	screen (on a pedestal or stand)
zhèng fǎn 正 反	front and back		xū shí 虚 实	perception; appearance
duàn dǐ 缎 底	satin background		xì xīn 细 心	care; attentiveness
sè jiē 色 阶	shade of color		nài xīn 耐 心	patience

专有名词

1. 非物质文化遗产　　/ fēi wùzhì wénhuà yíchǎn / intangible culture heritage
2. 蜀宫夜宴　　　　/ Shǔgōng Yèyàn / Banquet at Shu Palace

语言点

不仅……也……

思考

1. 请简单介绍单面绣、双面绣、异色秀和三异绣的异同。
2. 除了"芙蓉鲤鱼"和"蜀宫夜宴图",你还知道哪些蜀绣名品?请简单介绍一下。
3. 你的国家的刺绣里,有哪些代表作?请介绍一到两个。

参考文献
[References]

[1] 黄修忠 . 蜀锦 [M]. 苏州：苏州大学出版社，2011.

[2] 凸凹 . 纹道 [M]. 成都：四川文艺出版社，2008.

[3] 何鸿志 . 蜀锦史话 [M]. 成都：四川人民出版社，1979.

[4] 黄能馥 . 中国成都蜀锦 [M]. 北京：紫禁城出版社，2006.

[5] 赵丰 . 中国丝绸艺术史 [M]. 北京：文物出版社，2005.

图书在版编目（CIP）数据

成都印象／西南财经大学 汉语国际推广成都基地著 —成都：西南财经
大学出版社，2019.7
（走进天府系列教材）
ISBN 987-7-5504-3776-0

Ⅰ. ①成… Ⅱ. ①西… Ⅲ. ①汉语—对外汉语教学—教材②成都—
概况 Ⅳ. ①H 195.4②K 927.11
中国版本图书馆 CIP 数据核字（2018）第 241717 号

走进天府系列教材：成都印象·绣蜀绣
ZOUJIN TIANFU XILIE JIAOCAI:CHENGDU YINXIANG · XIU SHUXIU
西南财经大学　汉语国际推广成都基地　著

策　　划：王正好　何春梅
责任编辑：李　才
装帧设计：张艳洁
插　　画：辣点设计
责任印制：朱曼丽

出版发行	西南财经大学出版社（四川省成都市光华村街 55 号）
网　　址	http：//www.bookcj.com
电子邮件	bookcj@ foxmail.com
邮政编码	610074
电　　话	028-87353785
照　　排	上海辣点广告设计咨询有限公司
印　　刷	四川新财印务有限公司
成品尺寸	170mm×240mm
印　　张	46.5
字　　数	875 千字
版　　次	2019 年 7 月第 1 版
印　　次	2019 年 7 月第 1 次印刷
印　　数	1-2050 套
书　　号	ISBN 978-7-5504-3776-0
定　　价	198.00 元（套）